T0130356

Only You

Deeply from my heart

ELENA

© 2021 ELENA. All rights reserved.

No part of this book may be reproduced, stored in a retrieval system, or transmitted by any means without the written permission of the author.

AuthorHouse™ UK
1663 Liberty Drive
Bloomington, IN 47403 USA
www.authorhouse.co.uk
UK TFN: 0800 0148641 (Toll Free inside the UK)
UK Local: 02036 956322 (+44 20 3695 6322 from outside the UK)

Because of the dynamic nature of the Internet, any web addresses or links contained in this book may have changed since publication and may no longer be valid. The views expressed in this work are solely those of the author and do not necessarily reflect the views of the publisher, and the publisher hereby disclaims any responsibility for them.

Any people depicted in stock imagery provided by Getty Images are models, and such images are being used for illustrative purposes only.
Certain stock imagery © Getty Images.

This book is printed on acid-free paper.

ISBN: 978-1-6655-8627-6 (sc)
ISBN: 978-1-6655-8626-9 (e)

Print information available on the last page.

Published by AuthorHouse 03/01/2021

authorHOUSE®

Contents

Baby Angel

I gave birth to an angel,
beautiful, with sparkly blue eyes.
Even though my life was in danger,
I will never regret it in my life.

My angel was so beautiful and sleepy,
With golden hair and tiny little toes.
There were nights when you were weepy,
But I still remember that you liked playing with bows.

Minutes, or year after year,
Seconds, or day after day,
I love every time when you appear
And make me happy, and then I just pray.

I will always love you.
You are simply part of me.
I am more than proud of you.
You are the only one.

Class

Once upon a time there was a class,
A big class in a tiny room, but very brave and sure.
There were some days with a lot of fights and love.
There were prayers from many religions to God.
There was some time presenting our work to others.
There was a lot of dance with a lot of laughs with brothers.
I know you miss all the good and bad from that time.
I know we all get a bit fluffy by this time.
Remember only one thing, guys:
Stay safe and be alive!

Clear View

If someone does not really care about you,
Why you should care about them too?
Just forget about your feelings and love
Because in the end, you are not above.

Someone maybe hurt you by saying things.
Someone may convert you into lovely spring.
Someone may make you feel special today.
Someone may make you cry all the day.

Do you know what love really means?
Do you know that spring is all in greens?
Do you know what I know too?
Do you know there is no one good enough for you?

COVID-19

Coronavirus go away,
And never come another day.
I hope that all the people pray,
And everyone survives this day.

Woke up in the morning,
It's very early again.
Then nobody is calling.
Is scared, self-isolate.

I took my shower early
Then started to pray
For all the people in the world
To save their lives today.

Then go to take the train.
The people look at me.
My mask makes them feel scared,
But it is not only me!

Don't be scared of others.
Just protect yourself.
Protect your mums and fathers.
Protect the elders and someone else!

Daughter

Only you make me laugh.
Only you make me create.
Only you give me meaning to live,
my lovely and beautiful daughter.

You are sunshine to me.
You are air and water,
and I can't live a moment without you; I love you with all my heart and soul.

A little blue-eyed baby was born
with shaggy golden hair.
You looked, and I fell in love with you.
Oh, I love you more since the time you were in my womb.

For every day of these past seven years,
I thank you heartily for all the tears,
for every joy, for every moment next to you.
So far you are just amazing; I am proud of you.

I am happy that God has given me
the most beautiful daughter in the world.
So hearty, so kind and caring for me,
with purest heart and clear soul on the earth.

Know you are my joy.
You can make me laugh.
I love my life with you, just enjoy.
I will love you forever, even in eternity.

Do You Think?

Do you think you can break my heart?
Don't forget that I am special smart.
I can build up my confidence again.
I can really show you who I am.

Do you think it is good to play with girls?
Do you think you are the most special in the world?
I can tell you it is not good for you.
Whatever you did to them will return to you.

Do you use your knowledge and skills
To make them feel that you are lonely?
Do you know that all of them, if they appear
In front of you, then you will be in agony?

I don't care about your feelings
If you don't care about mine.
I don't care with whom you are living.
Thank God it is not me you decide!

Eternal Love

I just fall in love with you.
You make me feel so nice.
I just wanna be with you
Now and then, not only tonight.

The way you talk to me is kind.
When I look at you, I am shy.
The way you walk to me makes me smile.
When you sit next to me, I am in the aisle.

I feel so free and awesome.
You are just very handsome.
Just look in my green eyes.
I will love you forever; these are not lies.

Good Night, My Love

'Good night', you tell me, darling.
But it is not that good at all
If you are there, and I am here.
Reading the Bible will not help at all.

We are very sinful,
Very savage, and odd.
But also very love full,
With pure souls and good.

If the star is falling
I will make a wish.
Kiss me while it is snowing.
Love me as your dish.

I want to feel your lips
Under the falling snowflakes.
I want to hug you under this,
Even if my legs get frozen.

Love you as an angel.
Hug you as your mum.
Look at you like an eagle.
My love, please, please … come.

I Like You

I like the way you talk to me.
I like the way we start.
I like everything in you.
I more than like you so far.

When I look in your eyes,
I see how good you are.
I see your love and pain.
I see who you are.

I know you work hard.
I know you are awesome.
I know that you are a
Real man and handsome.

Just close your eyes.
I want to kiss them slowly.
Just hug me tight.
I want to sleep on your chest tonight.

Do you know me?
Please never again feel lonely.
Remember only one thing:
I am here for you only.

The Way You Talk To Me

I like the way you talk to me.
I like the way you look in my eyes.
I like the way you smile at me.
I like everything so far.
I like the way we find each other.
I like the way we start.
I like that you are honest.
I like that you are bold.
I like that you have self-confidence.
I like that you are smart.
I like the way we are.
I like you … so, so far.

Life of a Soldier

I meet you unexpectedly on one awful night.
You start to chat with me, and this is our start.
I chat with you, and I realise
That you are everything that I am dreaming about.

Then I look at your eyes; they tell me a lot.
I know you are kind and are strong like a robot.
You are smiling, but inside you
It looks like something is hurting you.

You know how to hold your emotions and stress.
You know how to push forward—
Even when the life has broken you—
Because you are strongest man in the world.

To be a soldier, to be a father,
To be all good things in the world.
Never forget from where you started
And why you are special in this world.

The life is crazy; trust me I know that too.
But that everything which doesn't put you down
Makes you stronger is true.
Hold yourself, be patient ... I do.

There are good days; look at them.
Never return to the bad way.
Look forward, be positive enough.
Then life will be ideal and ought.

Believe in God, believe in you,
Believe in punishment, believe in love too.
Believe in people, believe in truth,
Believe in everything you want; just know I believe
in you!

Little One

You smile with your little eyes
And look like you are talking.
Every day is new to you and me.
But I know you like to be walking.

Your eyes are like little diamonds.
Your hands are like magic sticks.
Your legs are faster than others'.
You are just little angel then.

I wish you a lovely childhood.
I wish you all the love.
I wish you good success in life,
Like your dad, and more.

Lost Soul

My life is a kind of magic.
My life is a kind of stress.
I don't want and I can't hide
my unhappiness and my sadness.

I wander and I don't find
my happiness in my days.
I don't know how to fight with my inner-self; even if I don't stop fighting, I burn inside loudly.

Whether I like it or not,
I wonder night and day of misfortune.
Can I just dress, or is there happiness somewhere for me too?

I hope to find it out soon.
I hope to fight with this.
Yes, but my life to have joy again
is not that easy with all the stress.

I want to live again,
to feel warmth in me.
I want to never stop laughing
and be reborn again, just me.

Messed-Up Life

One day I meet a guy
who makes me feel like I could fly.
One day I open my eyes
and see the reality behind.
One day I feel my life is broken.
I cry.

I make the most biggest mistake in the world.
I choose the most wrong partner on the earth.
Time cannot go back again,
So I have to pay for my mistake.
I cannot be the same as before.
I cannot help myself.
But trust me, I will love more,
And I will fight to be alive and brave.

I know that I am simple.
I know that I am bold.
I know that I have a dimple
On my face, and I am not old.

Just understand me as you wish.
Just love me as I deserve.
Just hold me as you can.
Just take me home.

Home is where your heart is.
Home is where your soul is.
Home is where your body is.
Home is where … you know … is.

The Right Way

If you find the way to my heart,
Please be careful with a special part
where my love and feelings are,
where nobody can steal.

The door was closed for both of us.
Please find the key and open for me.
I know I am overthinking, but please understand me.

My soul is hurt, there's pain, a lot.
Please fix it, help me, please.
Then kiss my heart and dream a lot
just for you and me.

The way you find, the way you see,
The way is there for you and me.
I wanna meet you in my days.
You know where is the right way.

Only You

Every day without you is lonely.
Every day without you is sad.
Every moment without you is so hard.
Every minute without you is bad.

Only you can make me smile.
Only you can take my heart.
Only you can give me everything.
Only you can; you are special smart.

I wanna kiss your lips.
I wanna feel your love.
I wanna dance with you like this.
I wanna feel your true love.

My heart is yours; take care of it.
My mind is yours; please look at it.
My body is yours; please love me, please.
I am yours; please keep me, please.

Pure Love

When I woke up, I was so happy. Do you know why?
Because I was dreaming about you all the night.
Then my day was almost at the end,
I was thinking of the time we spend.

I still can feel your lips on mine,
your strong arms around me,
your specific voice and sign.
My true love and you disagree.

Odysseus, you are intelligent and a real man
who plays no games and always makes a plan.
You are genuine, kind, caring, and rough.
Let me give you all I have, my pure love only for you.

Thoughts

Day after day I want to know more about you.
My hair will be grey if I don't stop thinking of you.
Who are you really? Please tell me.
I just wanna know that you care about my soul.

Love is happiness; true love is bliss.
Please be yourself and never somebody else.
If I hurt you by some words, please forgive me.
Don't be a stranger; that would hurt.
I wanna know you really!

True Love

True love has wings so I can fly.
True love is a gift from God.
True love sometimes make me cry.
True love is feeling like a hotpot.

My mind is telling me to stop again.
I should value myself in your mind.
My heart is forgetting who I am
When you kiss me from behind.

I wanna scream just from love.
I wanna feel you are serious.
I love you with all I've got.
I love you, truly love you, Odysseus.

Who Are You?

If you read as usual, which I am sure you do,
please be honest, and tell me the truth.
How many hours are you reading per day
without having any kind of play?

I know you love psychology; you know I do too.
Then make it simple, and tell me the truth.
I know you play no games; I know you love in some way.
I know you are intelligent enough, also very tough.

I still look at you and try to find the way
we both can be special and aware.
I still don't know everything about you,
so please tell me; just tell me the truth.

Who is hiding behind this lovely smile?
Who is laughing at my jokes just to be kind?
Who is scared to look in my eyes?
Who are you? Why are those lies?

You

You, smiling with your sparkly eyes
I know you are also laughing
Every day I want you to be mine.
Oh my love let's keep walking

My heart is beat faster
My soul is dancing along
My body is all sweating
My entire love is only yours.

I wish you a lovely night.
I wish you all the love.
I wish you good success in life.
I wish you to be mine, and I am yours!

You Can

Only the touch of your lips can make me alive.
Only the touch of your lips can make me cry.
Only the touch of your lips can make me feel hot.
Only the touch of your lips on just one spot.

Do you wanna feel my lips?
Do you wanna feel my love?
Do you wanna feel all this?
Do you? Tell me why not.

You can make me smile all day.
You can take me all the way.
You can tell me everything you want.
You can give me all I want.

Your Eyes

I was sitting on the bench.
You came and sat next to me.
Then looked somehow French
And a mystery for me.

I was afraid to talk
Until I saw your eyes.
Then everything is started,
Like we hadn't seen each other for a long time.

We walked for hours.
We smiled and talked a lot.
We ate together, habibi,
And then dreamed a lot.

When you kissed me for the first time,
I lost my mind.
I looked in your eyes.
I felt so, so shy.

Then I could not stop my feelings.
They just expressed themselves.
I fell in love with your eyes.
I fell in love from my heart.

I never felt so happy.
I never felt so well.
You make me feel like a real woman
At all times when I am with you.

To feel your lips on mine
Is just amazing; you know why?
Because you take my heart away, habibi,
And I am in love with you surely.

I like the way you look at me.
I like when you smile,
Then kissing you, and you make love to me.
I love you so, so far.

I see your eyes and dream of you.
I feel your eyes look at me too.
I touch your eyes with my lips, habibi.
I give to your eyes all of my feelings.

My Love

O, my love, I just love you in all the ways.
I don't care what the others are gonna say.
When I am in your heart and you are in mine,
Nothing and no one can tear us apart.

I been waiting for you all my life,
To find you the true love and be all mine.
I have been living just in the way of rife.
O, my love, tell me I am the one.

When I close my eyes, I can still see you.
When I move my hands, I can still feel you.
When you look at me, I can be alive forever.
When you love me, just love me whenever.

Printed in the United States
by Lowenkron

Printed in the United States
By Bookmasters